# All Aboard

## Doug Magee and Robert Newman

**All Aboard ABC**

# ABC

**COBBLEHILL BOOKS**

Dutton    New York

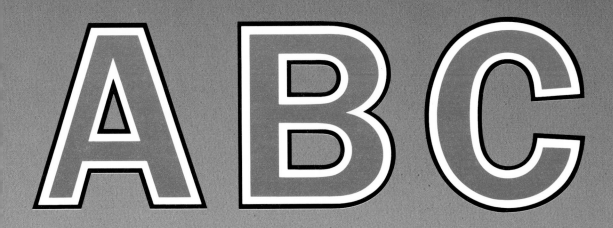

*For Angela, David, Eric, Maggie, and Tim.*

*We thought you could!*

Library of Congress Cataloging-in-Publication Data

Magee, Doug, date
  All aboard ABC / Doug Magee and Robert Newman.
     p.     cm.
  Summary: An alphabet book introducing the world of
  trains.
  ISBN 0-525-65036-9
   1. Railroads—Juvenile literature. 2. English language—
  Alphabet—Juvenile literature.   [1. Railroads—Trains.
  2. Alphabet]
  I. Newman, Robert.   II. Title.
  TF148.M34   1990
  625.1—dc20
  [E]                                   89-29852   CIP   AC


Published in the United States by Cobblehill Books, an
affiliate of Dutton Children's Books, a division of Penguin
Books USA Inc. Published simultaneously in Canada by
Fitzhenry & Whiteside Limited, Toronto

Designed by Charlotte Staub
Printed in Hong Kong
First Edition    10 9 8 7 6 5 4 3 2 1

Let's ride the rails from A to Z.

All aboard!

A a

## 68 Turbocoach

**Amtrak** trains carry passengers from city to city all across the United States.

**When the engineer pulls
these levers...**

**...the air brake stops
the wheels of the train.**

**B b**

The **boxcar** gets its name from its shape.

**Trains cross different kinds of bridges.
This is a trestle bridge.**

# C c

The **caboose** is the last car of a freight train, and is used by the train crewmen.

**A coupler joins cars of a train and holds them together.**

D d

**Diesel engines**
are powerful.
They pull
freight trains and
passenger trains.

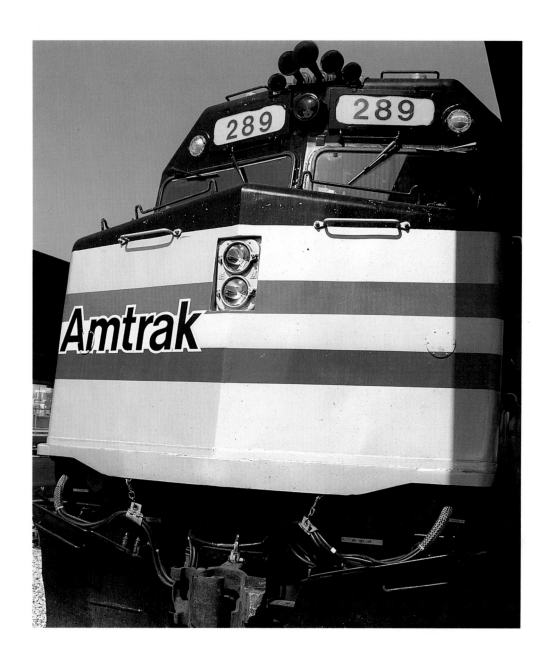

# E e

The **engineer** drives the train.

**He sits in the cab of the engine, at the control panel.**

**F f**

Freight cars carry nearly everything—

Canada

CPWX 608165

Government of Canada   Gouvernement du Canada

tank cars, coal cars

chemical tank car

hopper for grain

**coal, oil, grain, lumber, automobiles,**

**vegetables,
animals,
crates, boxes,
large containers.**

double container car

refrigerator car

**Freight cars have different shapes to do their jobs.**

lumber car

piggyback cars

# G g

UNION TANK CAR CO
UTLX 46705
CAPY 197000
LT WT 65900

**RAILROAD CROSSING**

**A grade crossing is where railroad tracks cross a road.**

# H h

The engineer sounds the horn
as the train nears a
grade crossing.

**Inside**, looking out, this is what the engineer sees.

**J j**

**A junction is where railroad tracks cross.**

# K k

**Keep off the tracks!**

# L l

The light lets the engineer see the tracks ahead.

M m

**Some passenger trains are run by electric motor cars.**

N n

**Trains need
lots of
numbers.**

O o

These freight cars are on an **overpass** above a busy highway.

**P p**

**Passengers** take trains to work and to play.

**Outside, it may be noisy. Inside, it can be...**

# Q q

. . . quiet.

**Rr**

Railroad tracks
are built on
a roadbed.

**S s**

**Signals** tell whether to stop or go, fast or slow.

**Springs** on a railroad car make the ride smoother.

**A switch moves a train from one track to another.**

**Tt**

**Rails are fastened to wooden ties in the roadbed.**

# U u

**Subways are trains that run underground.**

# V v

**Vents** bring fresh air into train cars.

# W w

Trains ride
on **wheels**
that fit
the tracks.

# X x

**X marks
the spot**
where tracks
cross a road.

**Stop, look, and listen before you start across.**

# Yy

Railroad cars are joined to form trains in a yard full of tracks.

**Z z**

Trains zip along tracks that look like...

...zippers!